My United States

Montana

JOSH GREGORY

Children's Press®
An Imprint of Scholastic Inc.

Content Consultant
James Wolfinger, PhD, Associate Dean and Professor
College of Education, DePaul University, Chicago, Illinois

Library of Congress Cataloging-in-Publication Data
Names: Gregory, Josh, author.
Title: Montana / by Josh Gregory.
Description: New York, NY : Children's Press, an imprint of Scholastic Inc., 2018. | Series: A true book | Includes
    bibliographical references and index.
Identifiers: LCCN 2017051025 | ISBN 9780531235638 (library binding) | ISBN 9780531250822 (pbk.)
Subjects: LCSH: Montana—Juvenile literature.
Classification: LCC F731.3 .G74 2018 | DDC 978.6—dc23
LC record available at https://lccn.loc.gov/2017051025

Photographs ©: cover: Gordon Wiltsie/National Geographic Creative; back cover bottom: ZUMA Press, Inc./Alamy Images; back cover ribbon: AliceLiddelle/Getty Images; 3 bottom: UrbanImages/Alamy Images; 3 map: Jim McMahon/Mapman ®; 4 right: Frank L Junior/Shutterstock; 4 left: jps/Shutterstock; 5 bottom: Paul Sawer/Minden Pictures; 5 top: Inge Johnsson/Alamy Images; 7 top: Karin Hildebrand Lau/Shutterstock; 7 center top: Patti McConville/Alamy Images; 7 center bottom: Granitepeaker/Dreamstime; 7 bottom: Greg Vaughn/Alamy Images; 8-9: Marg Wood/age fotostock; 11: Inge Johnsson/Alamy Images; 12: Carol Polich Photo Workshops/Getty Images; 13: Noah Clayton/Getty Images; 14: Chuck Haney Photography; 15: Jurgen and Christine Sohns/Minden Pictures; 16-17: John Elk/Getty Images; 19: Thom Bridge/AP Images; 20: Teguh Mujiono/Shutterstock; 22 left: Alan Cotton/Alamy Images; 22 right: railway fx/Shutterstock; 23 center: Paul Sawer/Minden Pictures; 23 top right:; 23 top left: Frank L Junior/Shutterstock; 23 bottom left: Donald M. Jones/Minden Pictures; 23 center right: jps/Shutterstock; 23 bottom right: Leonello Calvetti/Dreamstime; 24-25: Stocktrek Images/Getty Images; 27: Popperfoto/Getty Images; 29: The Granger Collection; 30 top: The Granger Collection; 30 bottom: Foto-Ruhrgebiet/Shutterstock; 31 top: Alan Cotton/Alamy Images; 31 bottom: Bettmann/Getty Images; 32: Kirn Vintage Stock/Getty Images; 33: Bettmann/Getty Images; 34-35: George Ostertag/Alamy Images; 36: Rachel Leathe/AP Images; 37: Walter Hinick/AP Images; 38: Danita Delimont Stock/AWL Images; 39: Stephen Simpson/Getty Images; 40 inset: EvgeniiAnd/Shutterstock; 40 background: PepitoPhotos/Getty Images; 41: Ami Vitale/Alamy Images; 42 top: Bettmann/Getty Images; 42 bottom left: Jason Davis/Getty Images; 42 center: Associated Press/AP Images; 42 bottom right: Splash News/Newscom; 43 top left: James Devaney/Getty Images; 43 top right: MARKA/Alamy Images; 43 bottom left: William Campbell/Getty Images; 43 bottom center: Gregg DeGuire/Getty Images; 43 bottom right: Agence Opale/Alamy Images; 44 top: Erik Petersen/AP Images; 44 bottom right: Zack Frank/Shutterstock; 44 bottom left: Radoslaw Lecyk/Shutterstock; 45 top right: Foto-Ruhrgebiet/Shutterstock; 45 top left: Cecilia Colussi Stock/Alamy Images; 45 center: Sean Xu/Shutterstock; 45 bottom: Chuck Haney Photography.

Maps by Map Hero, Inc.

Scholastic Inc., 557 Broadway, New York, NY 10012

1 2 3 4 5 6 7 8 9 10 R 28 27 26 25 24 23 22 21 20 19

Front cover: Yellowstone Club ski area

**Back cover: Entrance to the
World Museum of Mining**

Welcome to Montana

Find the Truth!

UNITED STATES

Montana

Everything you are about to read is true *except* for one of the sentences on this page.

Which one is **TRUE**?

T or F   Montana's state government is organized into five branches.

T or F   A gold rush began in Montana in 1862.

TREASURE STATE
7·09835B
MONTANA - 10

Find the answers in this book.

Contents

THE BIG TRUTH!

Bitterroot

What Represents Montana?

Mourning cloak
butterfly

Glacier National Park

3 History

4 Culture

Grizzly bear

This Is Montana!

CANADA

Kootenai
National Forest

Glacier National Park

Milk

John Deere
Tractor Museum

KALISPELL

Lewis and Clark
National Historic Trail
Interpretive Center

1

Montana
Historical Society

2

Flathead
Lake

Missouri

Fort
Peck
Lake

National
Bison Range

MISSOULA

GREAT FALLS

MONTANA

Western
Heritage Center

HELENA

Musselshell

3

Yellowstone

MILES CITY

Elkhorn
Ghost Town

BUTTE

Custer Gallat
National Fore

BOZEMAN

Granite Peak

BILLINGS

The World
Museum of Mining

Bighorn

4

Little Bighorn Battlefield
National Monument

IDAHO

Yellowstone National
Park Gateways

WYOMING

0   50
Miles

1 Flathead Lake

Montana's largest lake has 160 miles (257 kilometers) of shoreline and about 200 square miles (518 square kilometers) of water. Visitors love to swim, go boating, or just enjoy a picnic on the shore.

2 Montana Historical Society

This museum in Helena is a great place to learn about Montana's rich history. It has everything from Native American artifacts to historic mining equipment used in the state's earlier days.

WISCONSIN

3 Granite Peak

At a height of 12,807 feet (3,904 meters), the peak of this mountain is the highest point in Montana. It is a popular spot for skiing and snowboarding.

4 Custer Gallatin National Forest

IOWA

This sprawling forest covers more than 3 million acres (1.2 million hectares) in southern Montana. Visitors can hike and bike along the forest's trails or camp in the wilderness.

ORTH
KOTA

OUTH
KOTA

MISSOURI

There are more than 27,000 ranches and farms spread throughout Montana.

CHAPTER 1

Land and Wildlife

Just over a million people live in Montana, spread across 147,040 square miles (380,832 sq km) of land. This makes it one of the most sparsely populated states in the country. Instead of big cities and busy streets, it is a land of rugged wilderness. Fields, forests, and mountain ranges stretch as far as the eye can see. In many parts of the state, it is easy to explore for days without seeing other people.

Geography

The name *Montana* comes from the Spanish word for "mountain." All it takes is one quick look around Montana's wilderness to see how this remarkable state got its name. The snowcapped peaks of the Rocky Mountains rise up in the western half of Montana. They tower above the Great Plains region to the east. But even the Great Plains aren't flat. They feature gently rolling hills and many small mountains.

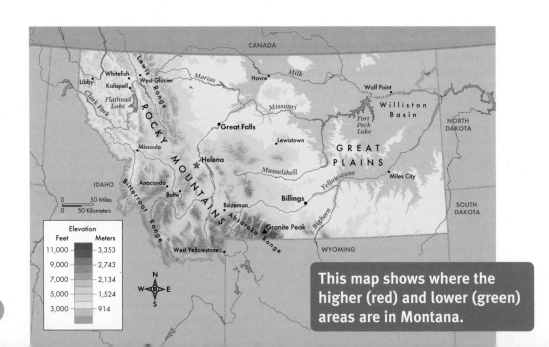

This map shows where the higher (red) and lower (green) areas are in Montana.

Glacier National Park

Glacier National Park is one of the country's most incredible natural areas. It covers more than 1 million acres (404,686 ha) of land in the Rocky Mountains of northwestern Montana. The park contains 762 lakes, 175 mountains, and a wide variety of plant and animal life. Millions of people come from around the world each year to hike, camp, fish, or simply enjoy the park's amazing views.

The leaves of many trees along the Yellowstone River turn beautiful colors in the fall.

Many rivers flow through Montana. The biggest include the Missouri River and the Yellowstone River. Their waters make Montana's land **fertile**. As a result, about two-thirds of the state is covered in farmland.

Montana lies at the top edge of the United States, with Canada bordering it to the north. To the west is Idaho, while Wyoming lies directly south. North and South Dakota form the state's eastern border.

Climate

Montana experiences a wide variety of weather, with warm summers and cold winters. Each region can be very different. For example, hundreds of inches of snow may fall on a part of the Rocky Mountains in a single year. East of the mountains, however, the city of Helena may receive just a few inches. In general, temperatures are warmer and more **precipitation** falls in the western part of the state. The east is cooler and drier.

MAXIMUM TEMPERATURE
117°F

MINIMUM TEMPERATURE
-70°F

As layers of ice and snow form on trees during winter in Montana, structures known as snow ghosts begin to form.

Plants

Thousands of different plant species grow throughout Montana's wilderness. Wildflowers such as lilies, poppies, and daisies add a rainbow of colors to the sprawling fields of the Great Plains. The state's forests, which cover about 25 percent of the land, have firs, pines, alders, and other types of trees. Tall, wild grasses make Montana a great place for animals to **graze**.

Many colorful wildflowers and tall grasses grow along the slopes of the Bitterroot Mountains, a range of the Rocky Mountains that spreads across western Montana.

Animals

Montana is also home to many kinds of animals. Enormous black bears and grizzly bears lumber through the state's forests. Speedy pronghorns sprint across fields. Waterways are packed with trout,

Though baby black bears are cute, people should never approach them. Their powerful, protective mothers are usually nearby.

bass, and other fish species. Mountain goats creep along ledges high up in the Rocky Mountains. Bald eagles soar through the sky, while rattlesnakes slither along the ground below.

The Montana Territory had two capitals before Helena: Bannack and Virginia City.

CHAPTER 2

Government

In 1875, when Helena was chosen as the capital of the Montana **Territory**, it was a wealthy town with an economy built on gold mining. Today, gold mining is no longer a major activity in the area, but Helena remains the center of Montana's government. Lawmakers from all around the state gather in this small city to make important decisions about everything from taxes to the state's school system.

Three Branches

Like other states, Montana's government is organized into three branches. The legislative branch is made up of a 50-member Senate and a 100-member House of Representatives. It writes and passes the state's laws. The executive branch is led by the governor and carries out these laws. The judicial branch is the state's court system. It interprets Montana's laws.

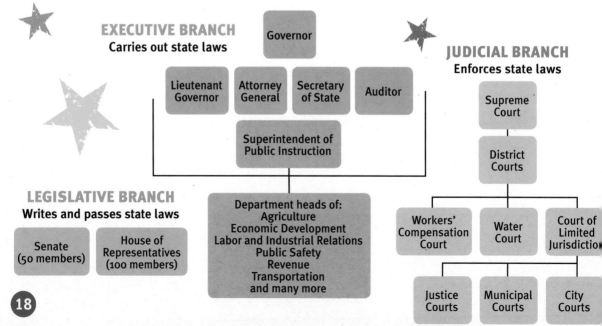

MONTANA'S STATE GOVERNMENT

EXECUTIVE BRANCH
Carries out state laws

Governor

Lieutenant Governor | Attorney General | Secretary of State | Auditor

Superintendent of Public Instruction

Department heads of:
Agriculture
Economic Development
Labor and Industrial Relations
Public Safety
Revenue
Transportation
and many more

JUDICIAL BRANCH
Enforces state laws

Supreme Court

District Courts

Workers' Compensation Court | Water Court | Court of Limited Jurisdiction

Justice Courts | Municipal Courts | City Courts

LEGISLATIVE BRANCH
Writes and passes state laws

Senate (50 members) | House of Representatives (100 members)

Governor Steve Bullock signs a bill negotiating water use rights with the Confederated Salish and Kootenai Tribes, a Montana Native American group.

Making a Law

The process of making a new law in Montana begins when a state senator or representative proposes a **bill** to his or her colleagues. After debating the details of the bill and possibly making changes, they hold a vote on whether to pass it. If both the Senate and the House of Representatives pass the bill, it is sent to the governor. The governor then decides whether to sign the bill into law or **veto** it.

Montana in the National Government

Each state elects officials to represent it in the U.S. Congress. Like every state, Montana has two senators. The U.S. House of Representatives relies on a state's population to determine its numbers. Montana has just one representative in the House.

Every four years, states vote on the next U.S. president. Each state is granted a number of electoral votes based on its number of members of Congress. With two senators and one representative, Montana has three electoral votes.

2 senators and 1 representative

3 electoral votes

With three electoral votes, Montana's voice in presidentia elections is below average compared to other states.

The People of Montana

Elected officials in Montana represent a population with a range of interests, lifestyles, and backgrounds.

Ethnicity (2016 estimates)

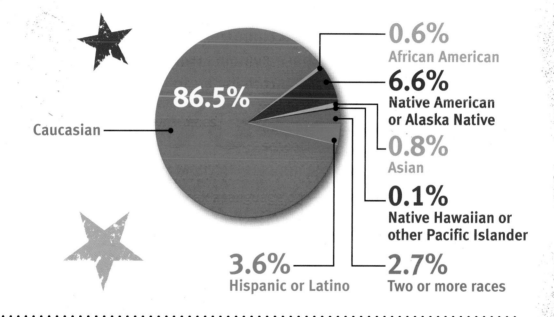

86.5%
Caucasian

0.6%
African American

6.6%
Native American or Alaska Native

0.8%
Asian

0.1%
Native Hawaiian or other Pacific Islander

3.6%
Hispanic or Latino

2.7%
Two or more races

93% of the population graduated from high school.

30% of the population have a degree beyond high school.

4% speak a language other than English at home.

67% own their own homes.

56% live in cities.

What Represents Montana?

States choose specific animals, plants, and objects to represent the values and characteristics of the land and its people. Find out why these symbols were chosen to represent Montana or discover surprising curiosities about them.

Seal

Montana's state seal shows many of the state's most notable natural features, such as mountains, forests, and waterfalls. The pickax, shovel, and plow represent the state's history of agriculture and mining. Along the bottom is the state motto, *"Oro y Plata,"* which is Spanish for "gold and silver."

Flag

Montana's official state flag displays the state seal in the center of a blue field, with the state's name across the top in block letters.

Blackspotted Cutthroat Trout

STATE FISH

A red marking like a cut along the lower jaw gives this fish its name.

Bitterroot

STATE FLOWER

The roots of this pink flower were once an important source of food for Montana's Native Americans.

Mourning Cloak

STATE BUTTERFLY

This butterfly got its name from its dark-brown wings, which resemble the cloaks people once wore to funerals.

Grizzly Bear

STATE ANIMAL

This enormous bear can be found throughout most of western Montana.

Western Meadowlark

STATE BIRD

This bird's distinctive call can be heard all across Montana.

Maiasaura

STATE FOSSIL

Many fossils of this duck-billed dinosaur have been discovered in Montana.

23

The fossils of many dinosaur species have been unearthed in Montana, including triceratops and maiasaura, both shown here.

CHAPTER 3

History

The place we now know as Montana has experienced many changes throughout its long history. Millions of years ago, it was home to ancient plants, dinosaurs, and other life-forms that are now extinct. Over time, weather and other natural events reshaped the land. Different plants began to grow, attracting different kinds of animals. Finally, by about 12,000 years ago, the first humans had arrived in the area.

Native Americans

The first people to visit what is now Montana were likely hunters pursuing large animals such as mammoths and bison. Over the following thousands of years, different people came and went from the area as the environment changed. Many Native American groups eventually settled there. They included the Blackfoot, the Crow, the Shoshone, the Cheyenne, and others.

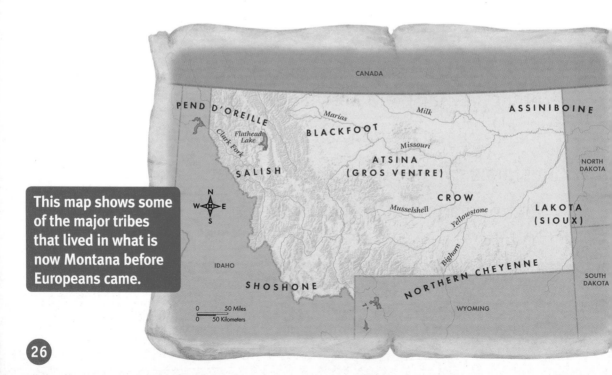

This map shows some of the major tribes that lived in what is now Montana before Europeans came.

Native Americans gather around a tipi in what is now Glacier National Park.

Most Native Americans in Montana hunted animals such as bison and deer, which provided almost everything the people needed. They ate the animals' meat and made clothing from the hides. Many people also lived in tipis. They built these homes by arranging poles in a cone shape and covering the cone in animal skins. Tipis were easy to move and set up. This was useful for people who traveled frequently as they followed bison herds.

European Settlers

In the 1700s, explorers from Europe began visiting the land that is now Montana. Many European nations had established **colonies** in other parts of North America, and they hoped to expand their control. Eventually, France claimed most of present-day Montana. In 1803, the United States bought this land as part of the Louisiana Purchase. The following year, President Thomas Jefferson sent a group led by Meriwether Lewis and William Clark to explore the land.

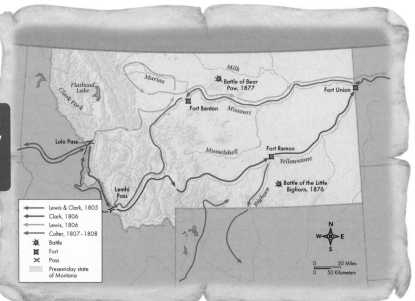

This map shows routes Europeans took as they explored and settled what is now Montana.

A Shoshone woman named Sacagawea helped guide Lewis and Clark in their journey across North America.

Lewis and Clark returned from their explorations in 1806. They reported that the West was rich in good land, wildlife, and other natural resources. Word spread, and people from the United States and elsewhere began moving west. Many hoped to become rich hunting animals for their furs. These fur traders brought diseases that killed countless Native Americans. By the mid-1800s, the traders had also greatly reduced the populations of many of Montana's animals.

Becoming a State

In 1862, gold was discovered in the southwestern part of Montana. Soon, new residents rushed to the area hoping to get rich. The population in the Montana region continued to grow. This helped lead the U.S. government to officially make it a territory in 1864. But as Old West settlers grew wealthy mining gold and other metals, raising cattle, and starting farms in Montana, Native Americans suffered.

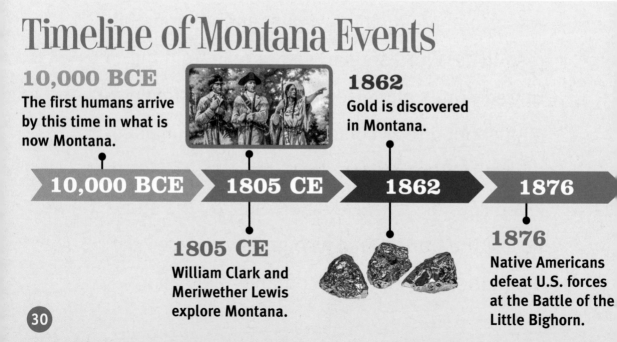

Timeline of Montana Events

10,000 BCE
The first humans arrive by this time in what is now Montana.

1862
Gold is discovered in Montana.

| 10,000 BCE | 1805 CE | 1862 | 1876 |

1805 CE
William Clark and Meriwether Lewis explore Montana.

1876
Native Americans defeat U.S. forces at the Battle of the Little Bighorn.

The U.S. government began forcing Montana's Native Americans onto **reservations** so white settlers could take their land. Many Native American groups fought back, leading to violent conflicts with the U.S. Army. Despite their efforts, Montana's Native Americans largely lost control of their homeland by the end of the 1800s. In 1889, Montana became the nation's 41st state.

1916
Missoula native Jeannette Rankin becomes the first woman elected to the U.S. Congress.

2006
Montana's largest wind farm begins operation near the town of Judith Gap.

1889 **1916** **1941** **2006**

November 8, 1889

Montana becomes the 41st state.

1941
Fort Missoula becomes a detention center for Italian and Japanese people living in the United States during World War II.

Miners rode trains deep into underground tunnels where they worked.

War and Peace

During World War II (1939–1945), Montana was home to a detention center. From 1941 to 1944, it held more than 2,000 people of Italian and Japanese descent. The United States was fighting Italy and Japan, and some feared these people would become spies.

After the war and beyond, Montana remained centered on mining, ranching, and farming. While it continued to be a land of small towns and wide-open spaces, its beauty and opportunities steadily drew more people.

The First U.S. Congresswoman

Jeannette Rankin was born in 1880 to a family of ranchers in Missoula. After earning a degree in biology and working many different jobs, she became an **activist**. She helped women win the right to vote in Washington State and Montana. In 1916, Montanans elected her to the U.S. House of Representatives. This made her the first woman to serve in the U.S. Congress. A lifelong leader, she fought consistently for women's rights and against war.

The Archie Bray Foundation for the Ceramic Arts in Helena displays huge sculptures made of bricks and other ceramic materials.

CHAPTER 4

Culture

From centuries-old Native American customs to the cowboy culture of the state's ranches, Montana has rich traditions. Many Montanans continue these traditions today. They play music, create art, and write stories inspired by the spirit of Montana. Residents and visitors alike can check out Helena's Holter Museum of Art, hike through Glacier National Park, or do countless other activities. All these things offer a taste of the state's unique culture.

Sports, Montana Style

Even though Montana does not have any major professional teams, there are still plenty of sports fans in the state. Montanans usually cheer for either the University of Montana Grizzlies or the Montana State University Bobcats. Few are fans of both because the schools are fierce rivals. People in Montana also love to root for local rodeo stars at events such as Wolf Point's Wild Horse Stampede or the Missoula Stampede.

The annual game between the Montana Grizzlies and the Montana State Bobcats is sometimes called the Brawl of the Wild.

Sled dogs sometimes wear special boots to keep their feet from freezing as they run along snowy trails.

Fairs and Festivals

Montana hosts fairs, festivals, and other fun events all year long. People in Deer Lodge celebrate the fall harvest with Pumpkin Sunday at Grant-Kohrs Ranch. This place is a National Historic Site that **preserves** the history of cattle ranching. As snow falls in February, crowds gather in Helena for the start of the annual Race to the Sky sled dog race. In August, hundreds of thousands of people head to the Montana Fair for food, rides, and more.

During snowy winters, workers at Yellowstone National Park use vehicles called snowcoaches to help visitors get around.

Montanans at Work

Montana was built on mining and agriculture. Many people in the state continue to work in those industries. Over time, the mining industry's emphasis switched from metals—such as gold, silver, and copper—to coal, natural gas, and other fuels. Today, tourism also provides many jobs. More people are visiting the state to enjoy its natural beauty and opportunities for outdoor activities. As a result, more workers are needed in businesses such as hotels and restaurants.

A New Source of Energy

Many people around the world are working to shift away from oil and coal toward cleaner energy sources, such as water and wind. As this occurs, Montana will likely become an important source of wind power. Its wide-open spaces make it the perfect place for large wind farms. On wind farms, many wind **turbines** are placed near each other to generate electricity from wind power. Today, wind power provides about 7 percent of the electricity generated in Montana. That number is expected to grow quickly. As it does, more workers will be needed.

A cow stands near wind turbines at a wind farm in central Montana.

39

Montana Munchies

There is plenty of good food to eat in Montana. Many locals like to hunt and fish. They grill up venison (deer meat) steaks fresh from Montana's forests and trout caught in the state's rivers. Montanans also love huckleberries. These sweet fruits grow in the wild in some parts of Montana. People pick them and use them to make pies and other desserts.

Huckleberry Jam

Ask an adult to help you!

Similar to blueberries, wild huckleberries are a prized treat in Montana. Turn them into jam and spread it on your favorite bread!

Ingredients
1 quart huckleberries
   (or blueberries), washed well
Water
5 cups sugar
3 ounces liquid pectin

Directions
Place the berries in the bottom of a pot and cover with water. Bring the water to a boil over medium-high heat. Stir in the sugar and let the mixture boil for about 2 minutes. Turn off the heat, then mix the pectin into the jam. Stir well, then pour the jam into jars before it cools down.

Some Montana ranches offer guided horseback rides along beautiful wilderness trails.

The Magic of Montana

From lifelong residents to first-time visitors, anyone in Montana can see it is unlike any other state. Life in Big Sky Country is often slow-paced, but that doesn't mean it's not exciting. It is a land of rugged adventure, where people rope cattle and explore the wilderness on horseback. Even as the world becomes more modern, the spirit of the Old West lives on in Montana. ★

Famous People

Ella Knowles Haskell

(1860–1911) was a lawyer and politician who became the first woman to argue a case before the U.S. Supreme Court. She lived in Helena and Butte.

Gary Cooper

(1901–1961) was an award-winning actor famous for his roles in films such as *High Noon* and *For Whom the Bell Tolls*. He was from Helena.

Charley Pride

(1934–) is a country singer-songwriter who has recorded dozens of hit songs. He has lived in Helena and Great Falls.

Evel Knievel

(1938–2007) was a motorcycle daredevil who was famous for jumping his bike across huge distances. He was a Butte native.

Barbara Ehrenreich

(1941–) is a journalist and activist who often writes about politics and culture. She was born in Butte.

Phil Jackson

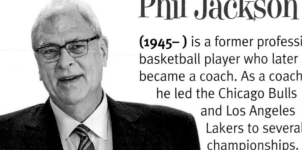

(1945–) is a former professional basketball player who later became a coach. As a coach, he led the Chicago Bulls and Los Angeles Lakers to several championships. He is from Deer Lodge.

David Lynch

(1946–) is a filmmaker, painter, and musician who is famous for directing films and creating the TV series *Twin Peaks*. He was born in Missoula.

Wilmot Collins

(1963–) is the mayor of Helena. He is the first black person ever to be elected mayor of a Montana city. Collins moved to Montana in 1994 from his native Liberia, a country in Africa.

Michelle Williams

(1980–) is an actor famous for her roles in films such as *Manchester by the Sea* and *Brokeback Mountain*. She was born in Kalispell.

Christopher Paolini

(1983–) is the author of the best-selling *Inheritance Cycle* series of fantasy novels. He is from Paradise Valley.

Did You Know That ..

Montana's all-time record low temperature, −70° Fahrenheit (−57° Celsius), is the lowest temperature ever recorded in the country outside of Alaska.

On average, there are about 7 people for each 1 square mile (2.6 sq km) of land in Montana. The only other states with a lower population density are Wyoming and Alaska.

Montana is home to seven Native American reservations.

One of Montana's nicknames is the Treasure State. It got this name from the wealth of gold, silver, and other precious metals found beneath its surface.

At just 200 feet (61 m) long, Montana's Roe River is often said to be the shortest river in the world.

Though most of Yellowstone National Park is located in Wyoming, a small part of it lies in Montana, including its original entrance.

Did you find the truth?

 F Montana's state government is organized into five branches.

 T A gold rush began in Montana in 1862.

Resources

Books

Bailer, Darice. *What's Great About Montana?* Minneapolis: Lerner Publications, 2014.

Domnauer, Teresa. *The Lewis & Clark Expedition.* New York: Children's Press, 2013.

Mattern, Joanne. *Glacier National Park.* New York: Children's Press, 2018.

Rozett, Louise (ed.). *Fast Facts About the 50 States: Plus Puerto Rico and Washington, D.C.* New York: Children's Press, 2010.

Stein, R. Conrad. *Montana.* New York: Children's Press, 2015.

Visit this Scholastic website for more information on Montana:

 www.factsfornow.scholastic.com
Enter the keyword **Montana**

Important Words

activist (AK-ti-vist) a person who works to bring about political or social change

bill (BIL) a written plan for a new law, to be debated and passed by a body of legislators

colonies (KAH-luh-neez) territories that have been settled by people from another country and are controlled by that country

fertile (FUR-tuhl) good for growing crops and plants

graze (GRAYZ) to feed on grass that is growing in a field

precipitation (pri-sip-i-TAY-shuhn) the falling of water from the sky in the form of rain, sleet, hail, or snow

preserves (pri-ZURVZ) protects something so that it stays in its original or current state

reservations (rez-ur-VAY-shuhnz) areas of land set aside by the government for a special purpose, particularly land that belongs to Native American groups

territory (TER-i-tor-ee) a part of the United States that is not within any state but has its own legislature

turbines (TUR-buhns) engines powered by water, steam, wind, or gas passing through the blades of a wheel and making it spin

veto (VEE-toh) to stop a bill from becoming law

Index

Page numbers in **bold** indicate illustrations.

About the Author

Josh Gregory is the author of more than 125 books for kids. He has written about everything from animals to technology to history. A graduate of the University of Missouri–Columbia, he currently lives in Chicago, Illinois.